ABOVE AND BEYOND

WITH

COMMUNICATION

ROBIN JOHNSON

Crabtree Publishing Company
www.crabtreebooks.com

Author: Robin Johnson

Series research and development: Reagan Miller

Editors: Rachel Minay, Kathy Middleton, and Janine Deschenes

Proofreader: Wendy Scavuzzo

Designer: Rocket Design Ltd

Photo researchers: Robin Johnson and Sonya Newland

Cover design: Katherine Berti

Production coordinator and prepress technician: Tammy McGarr

Print coordinator: Katherine Berti

Produced for Crabtree Publishing by White-Thomson Publishing

Photographs:
Alamy: CBW: p. 26, dpa picture alliance archive: p. 41t; iStock: RapidEye: p. 39c, MachineHeadz: p. 43b; NASA: p. 35b; Rocket Design: pp. 11t, 17b, 29b, 35t, 37b, 43t; Shutterstock: A and N photography: p. 23, Aleksandar Mijatovic: p. 4, Alexey Boldin: p. 11b, anfisa focusova: p. 6t, Becris: p. 24, bontom: p. 28b, c12: p. 15, Callahan: p. 20, Camilo Torres: p. 21, Cienpies Design: p. 45, DNF Style: p. 19, f11photo: p. 10l, FabrikaSimf: p. 25l, fontStocker: p. 30, HuHu: p. 34, iko: p. 39b, JStone: p. 6b, LEGEN -wait for it-DARY: p. 13b, magicinfoto: p. 9t, Marcos Mesa Sam Wordley: p. 37, mimagephotography: p. 10r, MR Gao: p. 27l, Mukhina Viktoriia: p. 41b, olegganko: p. 29t, PHOTOCREO Michal Bednarek: p. 17t, retrorocket: p. 5, Samuel Borges Photography: p. 12, simone mescolini: p. 31c, SpeedKingz: p. 36, Tetiana Yurchenko: p. 14, Thomas Amby: p. 40, Tushchakorn: p. 7, VLADGRIN: pp. 16, 18–19, 44, William Perugini: p. 33; Stefan Chabluk: pp. 5t, 13t, 22, 25r, 31t, 31b, 32, 39t.

All other images by Shutterstock

Library and Archives Canada Cataloguing in Publication

Johnson, Robin (Robin R.) ,author
    Above and beyond with communication / Robin Johnson.

(Fueling your future! going above and beyond in the 21st century)
Includes index.
Issued also in electronic format.
ISBN 978-0-7787-2830-6 (hardback).--
ISBN 978-0-7787-2844-3 (paperback).--
ISBN 978-1-4271-1834-9 (html)

    1. Communication--Juvenile literature. I. Title.

P91.2.J64 2016   j302.2   C2016-903301-5
                                          C2016-903302-3

Library of Congress Cataloging-in-Publication Data

CIP available at the Library of Congress

Crabtree Publishing Company
www.crabtreebooks.com   1-800-387-7650

Printed in Canada/082016/TL20160715

Published in Canada
Crabtree Publishing
616 Welland Ave.
St. Catharines, Ontario
L2M 5V6

Published in the United States
Crabtree Publishing
PMB 59051
350 Fifth Avenue, 59th Floor
New York, New York 10118

Published in the United Kingdom
Crabtree Publishing
Maritime House
Basin Road North, Hove
BN41 1WR

Published in Australia
Crabtree Publishing
3 Charles Street
Coburg North
VIC, 3058

CONTENTS

CHAPTER ONE

SPREAD THE WORD

Wake-Up Call

The alarm clock goes off. You open your eyes, groan, and pull the covers over your head. Outside, the bees are buzzing and the birds are tweeting. Inside, your smartphone is also buzzing with messages and tweets. Your dog is barking, and you wonder if anyone has fed him yet. You hear the phone ring as your mom calls you down for breakfast. You're not even out of bed yet, and your day is already jam-packed with communication!

What Is Communication?

Communication is the process of using words, sounds, signs, or behaviors to share ideas and information, and to express thoughts and feelings. You communicate verbally when you speak, such as chatting with friends, telling stories, or giving presentations at school. You communicate in writing when you post on **social media**, create poetry, and send texts and emails. You also communicate without using words. Your **body language**, facial expressions, and other nonverbal signals show others how you think and feel.

Hello

The Communication Process

Communication begins with a sender, or person who has something to say. The sender **encodes** the information they want to share. That means they put it in a form that can be transmitted, such as words or pictures. The sender chooses a channel of communication—such as speaking or texting—to send the message. A person called a receiver gets the message. They **decode** it and give the sender feedback. Communication is only successful when a message is received and understood.

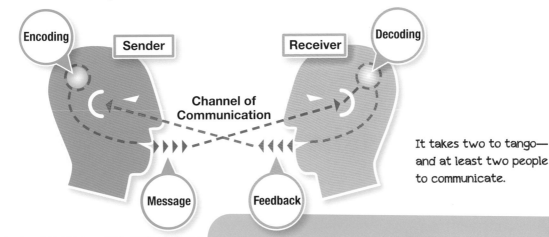

It takes two to tango— and at least two people to communicate.

There are many roadblocks to effective communication. Knowing what they are can help us avoid **miscommunications**.

21st Century Skills

Our digitally interconnected world is always changing and evolving. To keep up and be successful, we have to be lifelong learners, which means that we must be constantly learning how to think in new and innovative ways. The Partnership for 21st Century Learning is an organization that has identified four essential skills that students need to build to achieve their goals at school, at work, and in their personal lives. They are the 4Cs—**communication**, collaboration, creativity, and critical thinking. Each skill is important on its own, but combining the four together in our everyday lives is the key to success in a 21st-century world!

Born to Communicate

You might not know it, but you have been communicating since you were born. As a baby, you cried and fussed until your needs were met. Later, you learned to say simple words that helped you get what you wanted. You used finger paint and crayons to draw pictures. You learned the alphabet, and how to print your name and other words. Before long, you were writing down your stories and sharing your ideas. Now you sing, write notes, smile, make presentations, give high fives, and send texts. You communicate in all sorts of ways!

SPOTLIGHT

Malala Yousafzai changed the world—one blog entry at a time. In 2009, at age 11, she began writing about her life in Pakistan. Malala's family runs schools in their region. The Taliban—a terrorist organization—declared that girls in Pakistan should be forbidden from attending school. The young girl bravely spoke out publicly for the rights of girls—and was shot by a Taliban gunman for expressing her opinions. Malala survived the attack and refused to be silenced. She spoke at the United Nations, wrote a book about her life, and continues to inform and motivate people to stop injustice around the world.

"When the whole world is silent, even one voice becomes powerful."
Malala Yousafzai

Why Communicate?

People communicate to inform, instruct, motivate, and persuade others. To motivate means to give someone a reason to do something. To persuade means to convince someone to do something. We communicate in social settings, at home, at school, and at work. Communication helps us make friends and stay connected to them. It allows us to share our opinions and ideas at school, and work with others to achieve shared goals on the job. It shows others who we are and what we have to say for ourselves.

Sign Language

People communicate in many different languages. Some people who are deaf use Sign language to communicate. Sign language is a system of hand signs and movements that are used to convey meaning. Facial expressions and body language also help people who are deaf send their messages.

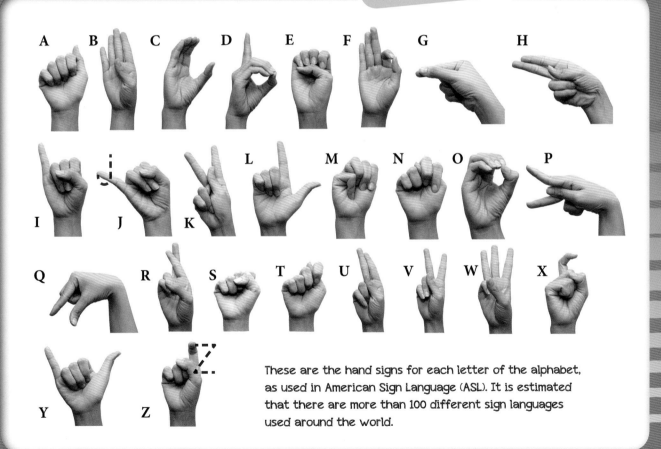

These are the hand signs for each letter of the alphabet, as used in American Sign Language (ASL). It is estimated that there are more than 100 different sign languages used around the world.

CHAPTER TWO

A BRIEF HISTORY OF COMMUNICATION

Rock of Ages

It was difficult for early peoples to communicate beyond their communities, since they lived without paper, telephones, or large-scale transportation. Instead, they used the resources available to them to share their messages and tell their stories—even long after they were gone. Early humans used soil and charcoal to paint pictures on the walls and ceilings of caves. The Inuit stacked rocks to form landmarks, called inuksuit. These guided travelers, and marked hunting and fishing grounds in the Arctic. In many Native communities, histories were passed on through oral stories and songs. These nonwritten forms of communication show what life was like in different early communities.

Brave New World

Over time, people developed new ways to inform, instruct, motivate, and persuade others. Paper was invented, which enabled people to record and preserve their histories in a new way—one that we still use today. The printing press allowed books to be mass produced and information to be shared widely. The telephone enabled people to exchange ideas and information instantly. Today, we communicate with people all over the world through the Internet. Each new technology changes the way people communicate.

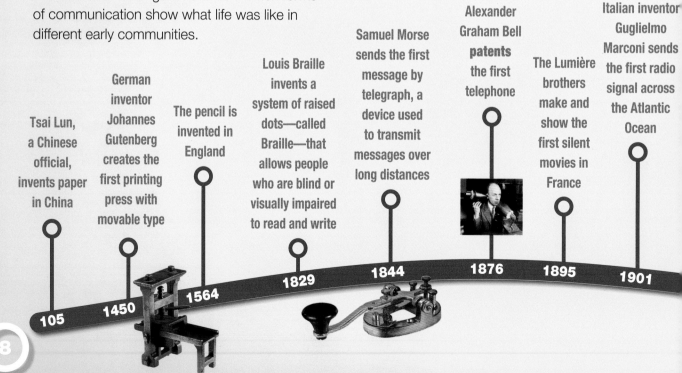

Tsai Lun, a Chinese official, invents paper in China — **105**

German inventor Johannes Gutenberg creates the first printing press with movable type — **1450**

The pencil is invented in England — **1564**

Louis Braille invents a system of raised dots—called Braille—that allows people who are blind or visually impaired to read and write — **1829**

Samuel Morse sends the first message by telegraph, a device used to transmit messages over long distances — **1844**

Alexander Graham Bell patents the first telephone — **1876**

The Lumière brothers make and show the first silent movies in France — **1895**

Italian inventor Guglielmo Marconi sends the first radio signal across the Atlantic Ocean — **1901**

Necessity Is the Mother of Invention

In 1825, American painter Samuel Morse received a letter that his wife was very sick. He rushed home and was shocked to discover that she had already died—and been buried! Morse was heartbroken—and angry that it had taken days to receive word by slow-moving horse messenger. Determined to improve long-distance communication, Morse got to work and later invented the telegraph. You might recognize his name from "Morse code," which is a system of long and short sounds or lights used to send messages.

Before audio technology was perfected, silent films were popular. Actors used body language and facial expressions to tell their stories.

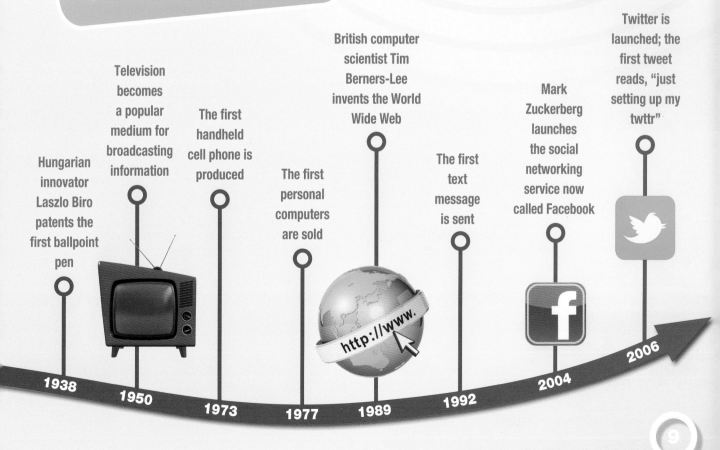

Hungarian innovator Laszlo Biro patents the first ballpoint pen

1938

Television becomes a popular medium for broadcasting information

1950

The first handheld cell phone is produced

1973

The first personal computers are sold

1977

British computer scientist Tim Berners-Lee invents the World Wide Web

1989

The first text message is sent

1992

Mark Zuckerberg launches the social networking service now called Facebook

2004

Twitter is launched; the first tweet reads, "just setting up my twttr"

2006

THE MODERN RACE CALLED A MARATHON COMES FROM PHEIDIPPIDES'S LONG RACE TO DELIVER HIS NEWS.

The Long Run

In the past, news traveled only as fast as people could carry it. Legend has it that a Greek messenger named Pheidippides ran nonstop from the city of Marathon to Athens in 490 B.C.E. He raced there—a distance of 25 miles (40 km)—with news of an important victory in battle. After delivering the message, the exhausted runner collapsed and died.

Word Travels Fast

Sending messages today is much faster—and far less tiring. **Digital communication** is now one of the primary ways we communicate with each other. You can pick up your phone, write out texts, hit "send," and away they go. You can snap a selfie and post it on Instagram. Within minutes, followers around the world have seen and liked it. You can meet and chat with friends on Facebook. You can blog, share, comment, instant message (IM), email, tweet, Skype, upload videos, download files, and use other kinds of digital communication—without ever breaking a sweat.

Digital Technology Use

United States

%	0 10 20 30 40 50 60 70 80 90 100
87	Desktop/laptop computer
81	Gaming console
73	Smartphone
58	Tablet computer
30	Cell phone that is not a smartphone

Canada (excluding Quebec)

%	0 10 20 30 40 50 60 70 80 90 100
93	Desktop/laptop computer
63	Smartphone
47	Tablet computer
35	Gaming console
18	Cell phone that is not a smartphone

This graph shows the percentage of 13- to 17-year-olds in the United States with access to digital communication technologies. Almost 90% of the teens surveyed use computers, while nearly three-quarters have access to smartphones.

This graph shows daily device usage for 9- to 18-year-olds in Canada. Combined use of laptop and desktop computers is more than 90%, while just under two thirds use smartphones daily.

#technology

Digital technology has expanded rapidly. People today have access to a wide variety of communication devices, such as smartphones, tablets, phablets, laptops, desktops, game consoles, iPods, iPads, and more. We have technology at our fingertips—and even on our wrists—24 hours a day. These devices have made it quick and easy to communicate with people around the world. Instant communication, a much wider **audience**, and the increasing amounts of information available online make learning effective communication skills more important than ever.

Make It Your Own

Compare your own experience to the data in the charts above. What kinds of digital communication do you have access to? Which forms of communication—digital or nondigital—do you feel are the most effective?

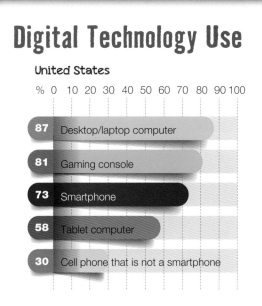

CHAPTER THREE

SPEAK YOUR MIND

Talk the Talk

Talking is such an important form of communication that we have many ways to describe our conversations. We make **small talk** and give **pep talks**. We **talk shop** and **talk turkey**. We **fast talk** and **sweet talk** and **straight talk**. We **speak out of turn** and **talk a blue streak**. We **talk tough** and **talk back**.

We talk and talk and talk. But how well are we communicating?

What Is Oral Communication?

Oral communication is the act of sending and receiving messages through spoken words. It is also called **verbal communication**. We use this type of communication when we have face-to-face conversations with individuals or groups, talk on the phone, **collaborate** with peers, and give speeches and presentations. Oral communication is important because it allows us to inform, instruct, motivate, and persuade others in a personal way. Our voices help show our emotions and intentions.

DO YOU KNOW WHAT EACH OF THESE PHRASES DESCRIBES?

Baby Talk

Babies bond with parents, siblings, and other caregivers through oral communication. Babies don't yet understand language, but they recognize voices and respond to baby talk. As we grow up, we learn to speak for ourselves and use words to say what we want. We build our vocabularies, and our communication skills become stronger and clearer. Before long, we are giving graduation speeches, winning debates, and having job interviews. We use oral communication throughout our lives to help us achieve our goals.

Hold the Phone!

In 2004, nine out of ten American households had landline phones. In 2014, that number dropped to only about half the homes in America, as more people switched to personal cell phones instead. Why do you think Americans are saying goodbye to their landlines? What are some of the pros and cons of landline and cell phone communication?

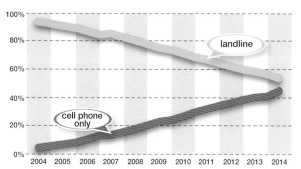

Canadians have been slower to hang up their landline phones, which may be due to logistics. The country's population is relatively low and spread out over a huge area, which makes it costly to build the **infrastructure** needed for cell coverage. This makes cell phones more expensive, and sometimes impossible, to own.

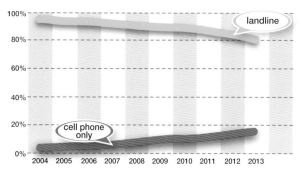

We have the urge to communicate from a young age. Did you ever use a banana as a pretend phone when you were little?

Talking Points

Like all methods of communication, oral communication has its advantages and disadvantages. This chart shows some of the pros and cons of speaking your mind.

Advantages of Oral Communication

- Oral communication is personal and can be private in some settings.

- You can adjust the volume and tone of your voice to reinforce your message.

- There is no delay in sending or receiving the message, and you know for sure it was delivered. Oral communication never gets lost in the mail!

- You can gauge the response of the receiver. Are they pleased or upset by your message?

- You can tell if the message is understood— and explain it further if necessary.

- The receiver can give you their feedback right away.

- You can discuss issues and collaborate to make decisions quickly.

- Oral communication gives you—and the receivers of your message—an opportunity to learn and practice attentiveness and **active listening** skills.

Disadvantages of Oral Communication

- Misunderstandings can occur if people do not hear your message correctly.

- You cannot plan, organize, or edit your words as carefully as you can on paper.

- Once your words are spoken, you cannot delete them or take them back.

- There is usually no record or proof of oral communication (unless it is recorded on tape or video).

- You can be interrupted or distracted, and lose your train of thought as you speak.

- You may feel shy or uncomfortable speaking in front of other people.

- It can be hard to deliver bad or unpleasant news face to face.

Words are like toothpaste. Once you squeeze them out, you can't put them back!

Have you ever played the telephone game? You sit in a circle, and the leader whispers a short message to the person next to them. The message is whispered from person to person, until the last person in the circle tells the group what they heard. It's usually been misheard so many times that it's completely different than the original message!

Materials needed:

A group of friends

Challenge:

Play the telephone game, but with a twist. Think of reasons why oral communication might fail in this activity. Then try to improve it and successfully deliver the message all the way down the line. Keep trying, and don't hang up the phone until the message is received.

One miscommunication can lead to another... and another... and another. Keep that in mind the next time you hear—or spread—gossip.

The Original Face Time

Interpersonal communication is the original face time. It takes place when we talk and share ideas, information, and feelings face to face with individuals or small groups of people. We use interpersonal communication at family dinners, when we work on group projects at school, and when we go shopping with our friends. Speaking face to face helps us understand a person's message and get to know them better. We can see the facial expressions, gestures, and body language that accompany their words. We can hear anger, excitement, sadness, and other emotions in their voices. We can shake their hands, and give them hugs.

The New FaceTime

Digital technologies have made it possible to get up close and personal—even from far away. Skype, FaceTime, and other video chat applications let us see, hear, and talk to people around the world in real time. They help us connect and stay close to friends and family across the miles. On the other hand, some digital technologies have made us less likely to meet and speak with people face to face. We shop, work on school projects, and work online, and we rely on texts, emails, and social media to deliver our messages. These communication methods are quick and effective, but they can be less personal than talking one on one.

"**Electric communication will never be a substitute for the face of someone who with their soul encourages another person to be brave and true.**"
Author Charles Dickens

Taking the time to speak personally helps build stronger connections between people, and results in fewer miscommunications.

Skype in School

Today's students can see the world without leaving their classrooms. The Internet, and digital programs such as Skype, let them listen to guest speakers and take virtual field trips anywhere. A program called "Around the World with 80 Schools" challenges students to Skype other classrooms near and far. The students ask and answer questions about their language, culture, and daily lives. They learn about geography, make connections, and discover the differences—and similarities—of people around the globe.

Talk to Me!

Teens' favorite way to communicate is:

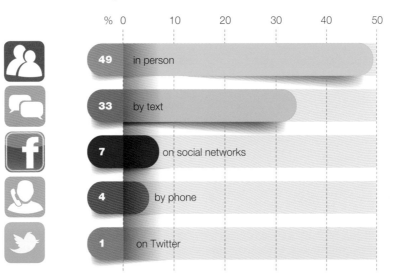

%		in person	49
by text	33
on social networks	7
by phone	4
on Twitter	1

Half of American teenagers surveyed say talking in person is their favorite way to communicate because it's more fun and easier to understand what people really mean.

Collaboration Station

Interpersonal communication is key when collaborating with others. To collaborate means to work together with individuals or groups to create or achieve something. At school, you might collaborate with other students to solve math problems, build science fair projects, put on plays, and make music. Using interpersonal communication, you can put your heads together and **brainstorm** ideas and answers. In the workforce, people also collaborate—often across the globe—to accomplish their goals.

Why Collaborate?

People collaborate because, as the saying goes, two heads are better than one. Collaboration brings together diverse people with different backgrounds, skills, and life experiences. Working together makes for a stronger project because considering ideas and suggestions from many individuals helps achieve the best possible solution. Working with others to solve a problem means that a lot of work can be divided among different people, and members of a group can motivate each other to work hard!

Tips for Effective Collaboration

- Make sure all group members understand and agree on the goals.
- Give everyone an equal opportunity to share their ideas.
- Listen carefully and consider everyone's ideas thoughtfully.
- Respect all opinions and ideas; don't argue, criticize, or interrupt.
- Be flexible and willing to **compromise** to achieve your goals.
- Divide the work and responsibility fairly among all group members.
- Value the contributions made by each member of the group.

Digital technologies have made it easy to discuss ideas and share information with groups of people around the world all at once.

Make It Your Own

Think of a time when you collaborated with others on a project. Were you a respectful, flexible group member who shared the work load? What strategies did you use to communicate with your group members? Analyze your own performance, and identify ways you could improve your collaboration skills in the future.

HANDS ON

This challenge gets you working with others to pitch a tent, and build your oral communication skills.

Materials needed:
A small group of people; A lightweight tent with flexible poles that don't need stakes

Challenge:
Pick one person to lead the group. Everyone else puts on blindfolds. The leader reads the instructions and tells the blindfolded people how to put up the tent. He or she will need to speak clearly, and direct the group step by step through the process. The rest of the group will have to listen carefully to get and follow instructions. And everyone will need to work together to communicate effectively and get the job done.

Once you've pitched your tent, work together to take the perfect selfie with it!

Going Public

Can you guess the number-one fear that most people have? It's not flying in an airplane, or even zombies. It's public speaking! Many people would rather face a zombie on an airplane than stand and talk in front of a group. There are all sorts of occasions in life when you might have to stand up and speak—speeches at school, weddings, award ceremonies, work presentations, and surprise parties, to name a few. And, if you want to become a teacher, politician, actor, lawyer, religious leader, or public figure, you'll need to master some public-speaking skills.

Talk of the Town

Many people feel uncomfortable being the center of attention in a crowd. The body reacts to this kind of stress in physical ways, by sweating and making your heart race. If you're nervous, it's important to find ways to relax your body before speaking to a group. Follow these tips to learn how to relax, improve your public-speaking skills, and become the talk of the town.

Public-Speaking Tips

■ Plan what you will say ahead of time. Stories add a personal touch and hold the audience's interest. Colorful language helps paint a picture.

■ Practice your speech, and make cue cards if necessary.

■ Your mouth can get dry when you're nervous, so drink water before—and even during—your speech. (But not so much that you need to run to the bathroom in the middle of it!)

■ Take some deep breaths to help you relax before you go on stage. Inhale through your nose, and hold your breath while you count to four. Then exhale slowly through your mouth. Relax your shoulder muscles.

■ During your speech, glance at your notes but don't read them word for word.

■ Make eye contact with the audience.

■ Use short sentences, and emphasize key words or ideas. Pause to give your audience time to think about them.

■ Say your words clearly and correctly. Find out how to pronounce difficult words and names before you start a speech or presentation.

■ Avoid using the words "um," "uh," "like," and "you know" to fill gaps in your speech.

■ Vary the tone, volume, and pitch of your voice. Speaking in a **monotone** will put your audience right to sleep.

■ Talk loudly enough for everyone to hear you, or people may miss—or misunderstand—your message.

■ Speak slowly. It takes time for the audience to decode your message.

This challenge gives you the chance to analyze and improve your oral communication skills.

Materials needed:

Computer, smartphone, or other audio tool

Challenge:

Use your audio tool to record yourself speaking. Make up some words on the spot, or recite the lyrics to your favorite song. Then play it back. Did you speak clearly, slowly, and loudly enough? Did you vary the tone, volume, and pitch of your voice? How could you improve your oral communication?

Talking is only half of oral communication. Being a good listener is just as important. We hear people talking all day long, but how well do we really listen?

Hearing is a sense that allows us to perceive sounds. It's not something we have to practice—it just happens. Listening, on the other hand, is a skill. It involves paying attention to a message so you can hear it, understand the content, then respond to it. It takes energy, concentration, and practice.

Stop, Look, and Listen

Active listening is a way of purposefully listening, decoding, and responding that helps us understand what is being said. It requires our full attention and focus on the speaker. That can be harder to do than it sounds! We are often distracted by other people, noises, and activity around us. We may not be interested in the subject, so start thinking about other things. We could assume we know what someone is going to say, so we interrupt or stop listening carefully. Or, we might start thinking about our response before the speaker has finished talking.

This list shows some of the strategies you can use to avoid communication roadblocks, and improve your active listening skills.

- Maintain eye contact with the speaker to keep your mind focused on them.

- Repeat the speaker's message—in your own words—to make sure you understand it.

- Use **reflecting statements** such as, "So what you are saying is…" and "So what happened was…" to clarify their message.

- Try to understand how the speaker is feeling and have **empathy** for them. Use phrases such as, "I understand that you felt angry when…" and "I see that you were hurt by…"

- Ask questions in a supportive way when the speaker pauses or stops talking. Don't interrupt them or jump to conclusions.

- Continue to give the speaker your full attention as they further explain their message.

- If you feel your mind start to wander, snap it back to attention in a hurry!

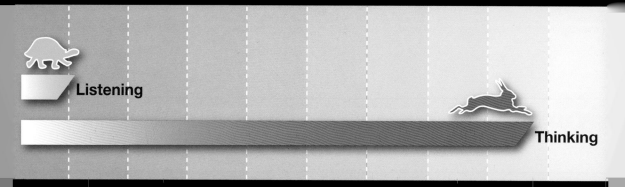

Listening

Thinking

We can think much faster t
minds often wander if we c

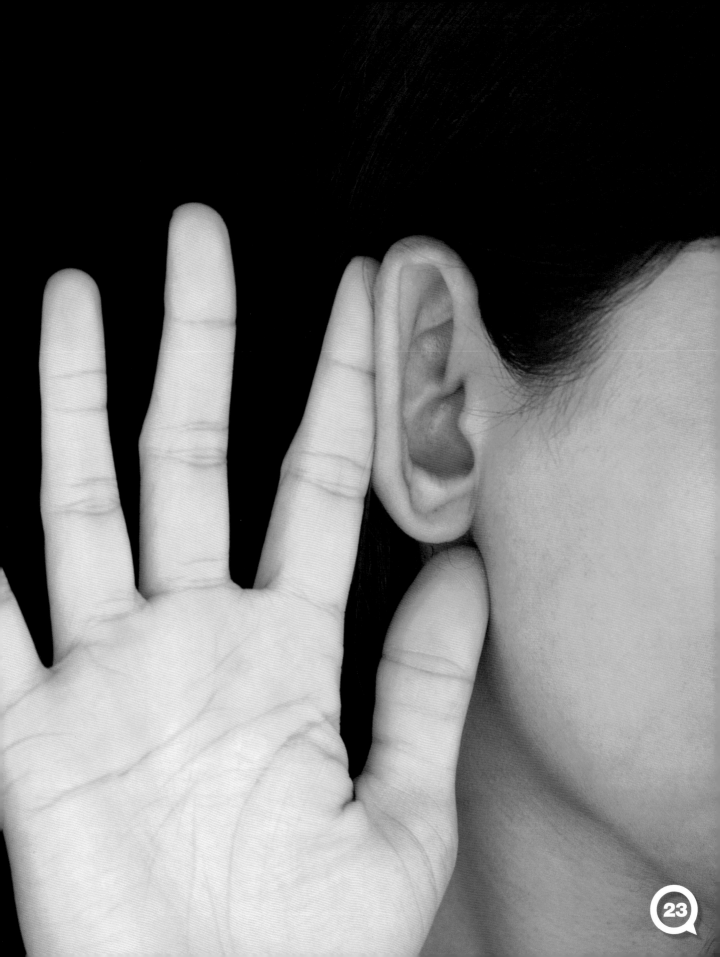

CHAPTER FOUR

WRITE ON!

Carved in Stone

People have been writing down their bright ideas for thousands of years. The ancient Egyptians developed a writing system made up of symbols, called hieroglyphs, that they carved on tomb and temple walls. The ancient Romans carved notices in Latin on slabs of stone and metal, and displayed them in public places. Over time, paper and ink were invented, which made **written communication** a whole lot faster—and lighter to carry. Today, digital communication technologies make it effortless to record and share our ideas instantly.

What Is Written Communication?

Written communication is the process of sending and receiving messages in writing. We use this type of communication when we write books, essays, and letters; send emails, texts, and IMs; and post blogs and comments online. Written communication is important because it allows us to record and preserve our thoughts and feelings. It also allows us to organize and edit our ideas so we can better inform, instruct, motivate, and persuade others.

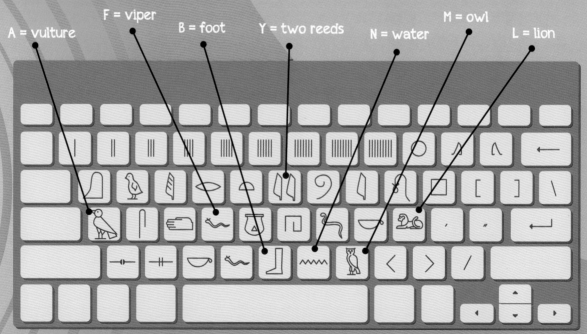

Ancient forms of written communication continue to inform us about the past. This picture shows the ancient Egyptian alphabet on the layout of a modern keyboard. Can you figure out how to write your name in hieroglyphs?

Advantages of Written Communication

- You can organize your ideas and choose your words carefully.
- You can revise and edit your work until it is just right before anyone reads it.
- You can provide more details and information than in a spoken conversation.
- You can express feelings and share news that might be difficult to deliver in person.
- Writing gives you a permanent record of your communication.

Disadvantages of Written Communication

- You don't know if your message has been received and understood.
- You can't use your voice or body language to show your emotions.
- Written communication is not as fast or personal as spoken words.
- Spelling and grammar mistakes can distract readers from your message.

THE INFORMATION AGE

We live in a period of human history called the Information Age. Communication technologies give us access to more information than ever before. In fact, we receive five times as much information today as we did just 30 years ago! Much of that information is transmitted through books, websites, magazine articles, and other forms of written communication.

Children Who Read for Fun Almost Every Day

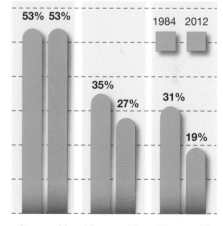

1984   2012

53% 53%	35% 27%	31% 19%

9-year-olds   13-year-olds   17-year-olds

We have access to more books, magazines, and other sources of information than ever before, but teenagers are reading for pleasure less and less. Why do you think reading is less popular now than it was in 1984?

It's a Long Story

Some forms of written communication, such as books, journals, and newspapers, are long. We use these types of written communication to share a lot of information or provide plenty of details. Nonfiction can teach us about history, detailing the facts of a single event or thousands of years.

Fiction takes time to set up scenes and describe characters to take us on winding adventures filled with plot twists and turns. Newspapers record breaking stories from all around the world to help keep us informed. Journals and diaries can hold a lifetime of thoughts, feelings, and memories.

SPOTLIGHT

Anne Frank was a Jewish girl who hid from the Nazis during World War II. For nearly two years, she and her family lived in a cramped secret **annex** in Amsterdam to avoid being sent to concentration camps. While in hiding, Anne recorded her thoughts, feelings, hopes, and dreams in a diary. Found after her death, her diary has now been published in more than 60 languages. It serves as an important historical record of how dangerous life was for Jews in Europe during World War II. Today, *The Diary of a Young Girl* continues to inform readers around the world about the Holocaust.

ANNE FRANK

THE DIARY OF A YOUNG GIRL

WITH AN INTRODUCTION BY ELEANOR ROOSEVELT

"The nicest part is being able to write down all my thoughts and feelings; otherwise I'd absolutely suffocate."

An excerpt from Anne Frank's diary

Writing Steps

Follow these steps to improve your essays, reports, stories, and other formal types of written communication.

1 **Pre-Writing** Brainstorm bright ideas and topics of interest.

2 **Drafting** Make a rough copy, where you focus on the content and order of information, not on the details.

3 **Revising** Rewrite and improve your work. Share it with other students to get their input.

4 **Editing** Check for spelling, grammar, and punctuation errors.

5 **Publishing** Share your work with your family and friends, or post it online in a safe space.

Raise Your Voice

Every writer has a voice that speaks loud and clear in their work. A writer's voice is their unique personality and point of view. It shows in the subjects they choose, and how they string their words together. Find your voice—then shout out loud!

Short and Sweet

Some forms of written communication are short and sweet. They're quick and easy to write—but contain enough information to get the point across. Short messages are useful when you're in a hurry or just want to deliver an informal message. They include postcards in the mail, grocery lists, instant messages— and lots and lots of texts!

There are 193,000 text messages sent every second!

Get the Message

More than half of all teens text their friends each day. Text messages are quick and convenient—and every English teacher's nightmare! Texts don't usually follow the rules of proper spelling and punctuation. They don't need capitals at the start or periods at the end. And they often use words that are abbreviated. These little messages are perfect for quick exchanges and lots of "LOLs"—but they can also cause big miscommunications.

Communication Roadblocks

Sometimes your texts don't send—but you think they did. Or your message autocorrects to something completely different than what you were trying to write. It's also hard to show your emotions and intentions in text messages. Are you being serious or sarcastic? Are you "JK" or really angry? Emojis can help show your feelings, but winky faces and thumbs up can only do so much. Checking your messages before you send them and following up with another form of communication—such as a phone call or FaceTime—can help prevent texting troubles.

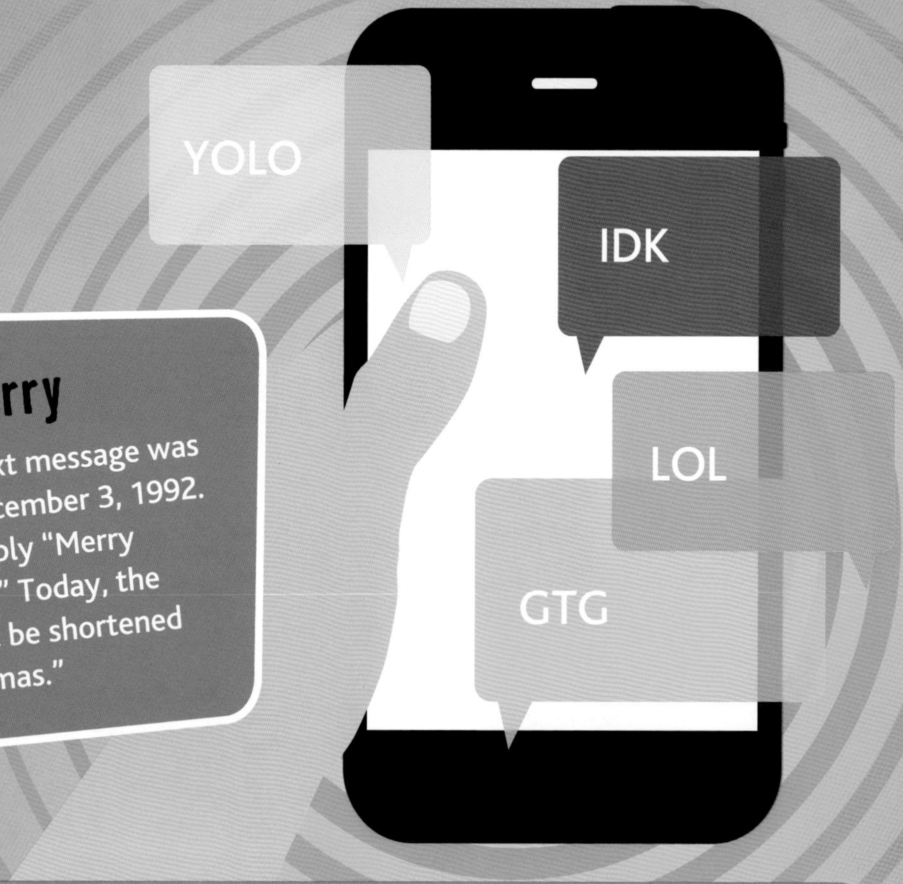

YOLO

IDK

LOL

GTG

Very Merry

The first text message was sent on December 3, 1992. It read simply "Merry Christmas." Today, the text might be shortened to "mry xmas."

Why Teens Like Texting

This graph shows the reasons some teens prefer to send texts more than other forms of communication.

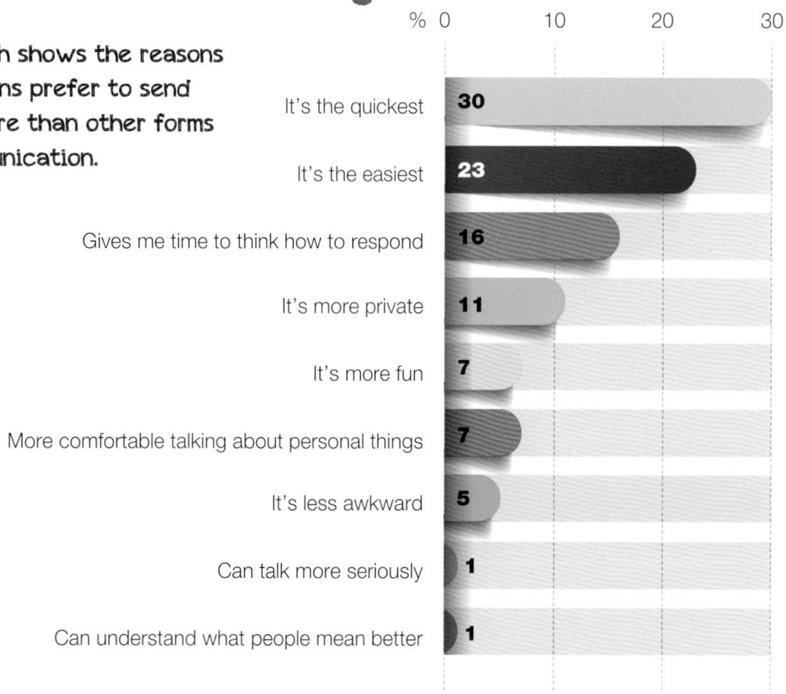

%	0	10	20	30

Reason	Percentage
It's the quickest	30
It's the easiest	23
Gives me time to think how to respond	16
It's more private	11
It's more fun	7
More comfortable talking about personal things	7
It's less awkward	5
Can talk more seriously	1
Can understand what people mean better	1

CHAPTER FIVE

PICTURE THIS

Visual Communication

Sometimes speaking or writing our messages doesn't show the whole picture—and that's where **visual communication** comes in. Visual communication is sharing ideas and information through visual aids, such as photos, symbols, drawings, videos, maps, signs, and cartoons. Visuals enhance oral and written communications. When you add a picture to spoken words or text, your message will be more powerful.

Get the Picture

Adding visual communication to a presentation at school or work helps focus the listener's attention on what you're saying. You can make memes or add emojis to clarify or draw attention to your texts. You can use models in your science fair project to help your audience better understand a complicated process. Images on road signs and public restrooms can help direct you in countries where you don't speak the language. Even this book about communication uses pictures, bar graphs, pie charts, timelines, infographics, and all sorts of visuals to aid understanding and keep your interest!

> **"Of all of our inventions for mass communication, pictures still speak the most universally understood language."**
>
> *Walt Disney*

10%   20%   80%

Seeing is believing—and remembering! People remember just 10 percent of what they hear and 20 percent of what they read, but 80 percent of what they see and do.

If you've ever followed building instructions, you know the importance of visual communication!

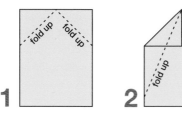

1   2   3   4

fold sides down
(in opposite directions)

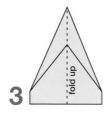

5

People who follow directions that have both text and illustrations do 323 percent better than people following directions with text alone.

Look and Learn

Not all visuals are created equal. Follow these tips to make your graphs, maps, and diagrams picture perfect!

Choose a visual aid that will enhance your message. Pie charts and pictures of pies serve very different purposes!

Use the right visual for the situation. You wouldn't build a 3-D model to give someone directions, but models are ideal for showing how volcanoes erupt and engines work.

Present your content in a simple, logical, and organized way.

Avoid crowding too much information in your visual aid, or it will become cluttered and confusing.

Use eye-catching colors. They make the information pop and catch the audience's attention. But using too many different colors might distract from your message.

Use simple, readable fonts if the visual includes text.

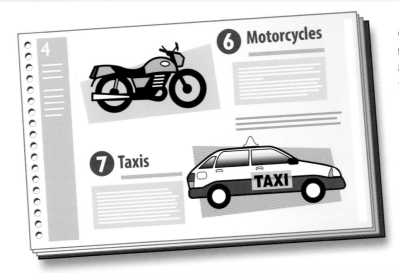

Color visuals make people 80 percent more willing to read.

SPOTLIGHT

For educator Salman Khan, there is more to YouTube than music and cat videos! In 2006, he created Khan Academy. The nonprofit organization posts short lessons on YouTube about math, science, history, and other subjects. The videos feature step-by-step doodles, diagrams, models, and other visual aids. Khan created the platform so people everywhere would have access to a free, world-class education. Today, the videos have been viewed more than 784 million times.

The Big Picture

Instagram, YouTube, Vine, and other media-sharing services, give us access to vast amounts of visual information. Anyone can see and publish pictures, videos, songs, memes, and other visuals, at any time.

What are the pros and cons of having instant access to an international audience, and an endless stream of content?

MORE THAN 1 MILLION SELFIES ARE TAKEN EACH DAY!

CHAPTER SIX

SOCIAL STUDIES

#socialmedia

What do Facebook, Instagram, Twitter, Snapchat, Google+, Vine, and Tumblr, all have in common? They're all social media platforms for virtual communities that require us to create online profiles to join. Social media allows us to connect with people, exchange ideas, and share information across the Internet—but it takes up a lot of our free time! The average teen spends more than an hour using social media each day.

Tools of the Trade

Social media is a powerful communication tool. It gives us access to an international audience with the touch of a key, and allows us to keep in touch with our friends and families, as well as make new friends. It lets us bond with people around the globe who share our interests and points of view. It also exposes us to new ideas and diverse opinions. Social media makes the whole wide world seem a little bit smaller—and a lot more social.

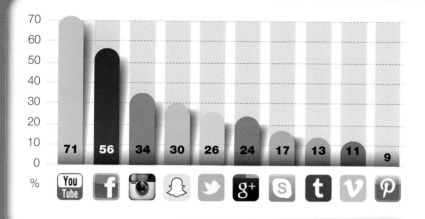

Social Media Usage in Canada

This graph shows the top social sharing sites used by 9- to 18-year-olds in Canada (excluding Quebec). Nearly three-quarters use YouTube and more than half use Facebook.

SPOTLIGHT

Commander Chris Hadfield is a Canadian astronaut who became an out-of-this-world social media sensation. In 2013, he spent five months at the International Space Station. While there, Hadfield posted on Facebook, Reddit, and Tumblr. He tweeted pictures of Earth each day. He even recorded David Bowie's song "Space Oddity" in space, which now has more than 30 million views on YouTube. Hadfield used social media to get people interested in space travel, and his message was heard around the planet.

Short and Tweet

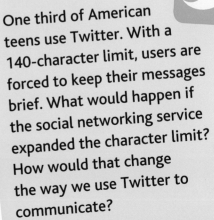

One third of American teens use Twitter. With a 140-character limit, users are forced to keep their messages brief. What would happen if the social networking service expanded the character limit? How would that change the way we use Twitter to communicate?

> **"What we're doing on the Space Station is fundamentally fascinating. And I think the evidence shows through a measure like Twitter."**
> *Commander Chris Hadfield*

Fast and Furious

Word travels fast on social media. Posts, pictures, and videos can spread like wildfire. Some even **go viral**. That means they quickly become wildly popular as more and more people "like" and share them online. Reaching a wide audience fast can be useful for good causes. It helps police find missing children. It lets leaders communicate their views and get input from voters. It helps charities raise funds and awareness for their causes.

Speak No Evil

However, not everything that circulates on social media is positive. Bad news and hurtful gossip spread just as fast—or even faster—than good news. **Cyberbullying** is a common practice on social media. It is the act of using digital communication to harm or bully other people. People sometimes write mean comments, post embarrassing pictures and videos, and spread vicious rumors. Because social media is so widespread, it can be hard to escape this type of bullying. But help—and new friends and followers—are always just a click away.

Face the Nation

There are more than 1 billion Facebook users. If they all formed a country, it would have the largest population in the world!

The pen is mightier than the sword—and your words can cut deep. Never use social media to post comments, pictures, or videos that could hurt other people.

Buckets of Money

In August 2014, the Ice Bucket Challenge went viral on social media. Millions of people poured buckets of ice water over their heads to raise awareness—and research money—for a disease called ALS. The campaign was a huge success, raising a cool $115 million for the cause.

This chart shows that most teens feel more connected to their friends via social media. Do you feel the same way?

	A lot better connected	A little better connected	Not better connected
To friends' feelings	20%	49%	30%
To friends' lives	33%	50%	17%

CHAPTER SEVEN

MORE THAN WORDS CAN SAY

Speak Volumes

You have learned how to speak clearly and choose your words and images carefully. But when it comes to communication, actions can speak louder than words. When you wrinkle up your nose, your disgust is as plain as the nose on your face. When you roll your eyes, it's easy to see that you're not impressed. On the other hand, nods and thumbs up show your silent approval. We can speak volumes—without even saying a word!

Face Value

We use visual cues to help us understand what other people are thinking and feeling. There are 21 different facial expressions that people around the world use and recognize. We all show happiness, sadness, anger, fear, disgust, and surprise—as well as combinations of those six basic emotions—the same way. Does that surprise you? When we are not communicating in person, images such as emojis help us communicate to the receiver what we are feeling.

Without a Word

Nonverbal communication is all the wordless cues we send and receive each day. It includes body language such as your posture and **mannerisms**. Facial expressions, such as grinning, frowning, and raising your eyebrows, are also part of nonverbal communication. Learning the meanings of these unspoken signals—both good and bad—can help you communicate more effectively.

Born This Way

People have an **innate** ability to communicate. In other words, we are born communicators. No one teaches babies to smile, shed tears, or spit out their green beans! We are born knowing how to blink, blush, flinch, sweat, and react to others in all sorts of ways. As we grow up, we watch, learn, and imitate the body language that is used in our cultures. Shrugging our shoulders shows that we haven't got a clue. Waving our hands is one way of saying hello. We use these learned types of nonverbal communication every day. But we also send all sorts of messages without even knowing it.

ACTIONS CAN SPEAK LOUDER THAN WORDS

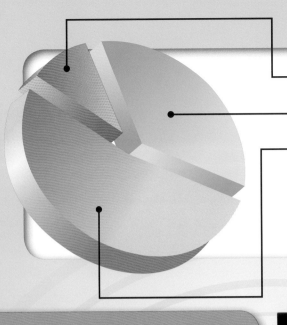

Words account for **7%**

Tone of voice accounts for **38%**

Body language accounts for **55%**

Words convey only a small part of your message. In fact, some experts say that body language makes up more than half of all communication!

This activity challenges you to interpret body language without verbal cues.

Materials needed:
A television

Challenge:
The next time you watch TV, turn off the sound for a few minutes. Study the body language of the people you see. What messages do you think their gestures and facial expressions are sending?

HANDS ON

Proof Positive

We send nonverbal messages all day long. Some of the messages are positive. They reinforce our words and make us more believable. If we say we're fascinated with a topic, we'll also lean in closer so we don't miss a word. If we say we agree with a decision, we'll also nod. Our nonverbal communication matches—and strengthens—our verbal communication.

Mixed Messages

Some of the nonverbal messages we send are negative. They show that we're bored, angry, or defensive. We may insist that we're open to discussion, but our crossed arms and legs show otherwise. We may say that we're interested, but then slouch, fidget, tap our feet, and play with our hair—all signs of boredom. Our body language can contradict our words, and be roadblocks to effective communication.

Do...

Make eye contact to show you're interested and engaged.

Do...

Use hand gestures in conversation. Showing open palms suggests that you're being honest and have nothing to hide.

Do...

Sit or stand up straight, with your shoulders relaxed and your arms at your sides. That makes you look open and confident. Lean forward slightly to show interest.

Do...

Pay attention to your feet. They point in the direction you really want to go—and can show that you want to leave the conversation.

Do...

Mirror another person's facial expressions and body language. This creates a bond between you and shows that you feel the same way they do.

Don't...

Avoid eye contact when you're talking to someone. That suggests you're nervous or being dishonest.

Don't...

Put your hands in your pockets or behind your back. This suggests that you are hiding information or not telling the truth.

Don't...

Slouch or lean back in your chair. That makes you look bored or indifferent. But don't lean too far forward either. That can make you look aggressive.

Don't...

Tap or jiggle your feet. That shows you are nervous or bored.

Don't...

Copy someone's body language to be mean or make fun of them.

SPOTLIGHT

Steve Jobs was a master of communication. The cofounder of Apple Inc. gave inspiring presentations to launch the company's newest digital products. Customers eagerly looked forward to these presentations. Jobs was enormously persuasive in his speeches, but his body language also showed he was cool, casual, and confident. Jobs kept eye contact with the audience. His frequent hand gestures were natural and relaxed. His posture showed he was open to the audience—he rarely stood behind a podium, crossed his arms, or put his hands in his pockets. Jobs well done!

These fingers are using body language to communicate!

41

CHAPTER EIGHT

LAST CALL

Choose Wisely

Choosing the right method of communication can make or break your message. But how do you decide if you should speak, write, or send your message—complete with smiley emojis—digitally? For example, if you are running late to meet a friend you might send them a quick text, but you wouldn't submit a school report or apply for a job by text message!

Choosing your method of communication depends on several factors, including:

- Is the purpose of your message to persuade, instruct, inform, or motivate your audience?
- Where is the audience located?
- Do you need a quick response?

The Rules

These general rules will help you decide which communication method to use so your audience gets the message loud and clear. Remember there is some overlap: for example, emails are both written and digital types of communication.

Oral Communication

Use oral communication, such as talking in person, on the phone, or on FaceTime, when:

- Your message is simple or straightforward
- You want to use your tone of voice, facial expressions, and body language to show the emotion behind your message
- You want immediate (verbal or nonverbal) feedback from your audience
- You want to encourage discussion, to help solve a problem, for example
- You can easily reach or meet with your audience

Written Communication

Use written communication, including essays, letters, and job applications, when:

- Your message is complex
- You want a record of your communication
- It is a formal situation, such as a school or work assignment
- You need to communicate with a large audience who may be far away
- You don't need to gauge your audience's reaction or get immediate feedback

Digital Communication

Use digital communication, such as text messages and emails, when:

- You need to send your message quickly
- You are communicating with people in different locations
- You want to include audio and/or video in your message
- You want to allow others to add their input

This chart shows how and how often American teens communicate with their friends. More than half the teens surveyed text their friends each day. IM is the second most common method of daily communication, followed closely by talking in person.

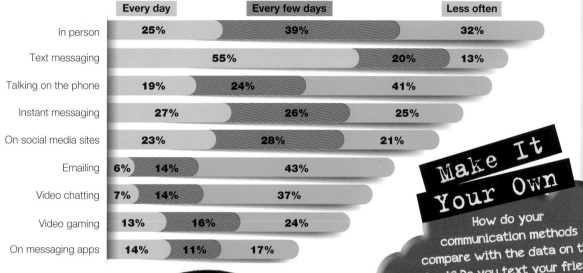

	Every day	Every few days	Less often
In person	25%	39%	32%
Text messaging	55%	20%	13%
Talking on the phone	19%	24%	41%
Instant messaging	27%	26%	25%
On social media sites	23%	28%	21%
Emailing	6%	14%	43%
Video chatting	7%	14%	37%
Video gaming	13%	16%	24%
On messaging apps	14%	11%	17%

Make It Your Own

How do your communication methods compare with the data on this chart? Do you text your friends every day? Or do you prefer to communicate via social media, talking on the phone, or through other methods? How does your audience change your choice of communication method?

Get Smart

When Alexander Graham Bell invented the telephone in 1876, he could never have imagined how smart our phones would become. Today, there's an app for this and an app for that. We fling angry birds, crush candies, and play online games with people around the world. We use our phones to control the temperature and lights in our homes—and to send messages to family members in the next room. We measure our heart rates with our phones—and check that our friends liked our posts and pics. And sometimes we even use our phones to make phone calls!

The Future Is Friendly

New technologies have changed the way we communicate. We have instant access to a worldwide audience that is bombarded with information every day. This makes effective oral, written, and digital communication more important than ever. There are endless channels to send our messages—and billions of people ready to receive them. Rapidly changing technology ensures that communication will continue to change and evolve in the future, and learning communication skills is a lifelong challenge. You have what it takes—so what do you have to say for yourself?

Make It Your Own

Think of a time when communication failed. Maybe you had an argument and could not understand each other's point of view. Maybe a text didn't go through and your BFF didn't know you canceled plans. If you could go back in time, how could you turn the miscommunication into successful communication?

Communication Checklist

Use this checklist to make sure you've covered your communication bases.

- Do you know the purpose of your message?
- Is your message clear, concise, colorful, and complete?
- Have you checked for errors in your message?
- Have you chosen the most effective channel to send your message?
- Are you sending your message to the right audience?

Top 5 Career Skills

These are the top skills employers look for when they hire people. Communication is number one, followed by organizational skills and writing. Use your written communication skills to get a job interview, and your oral communication skills to impress the employer. Then use all your communication skills on the job!

1 Communication Skills

2 Organizational Skills

3 Writing

4 Customer Service

5 Problem-Solving

GLOSSARY

active listening A way of listening, decoding, and responding that helps you understand a message clearly

annex A room or part of a building that is separate from the main building

audience The people who watch, read, or listen to something

body language Movements or positions of the body that show a person's thoughts or feelings

brainstorm To quickly come up with and record ideas without judging them, often in a group

collaborate To work together to create or achieve something

compromise To reach an agreement by each person giving up something they wanted

cyberbullying Using digital communication to send or post hurtful messages, pictures, or videos

decode To figure out what a message means

digital communication Using computers, phones, and other technologies to send and receive messages

empathy The ability to understand and share someone else's feelings

encodes Puts a message in a form, such as words or images, that can be shared

go viral To spread quickly on the Internet as more and more people share a picture, video, or other message

infrastructure The basic equipment and structures needed to function properly

innate Existing from the time a person is born

interpersonal communication Sharing ideas, information, and feelings face to face with individuals or small groups of people

mannerism Things a person does repeatedly with their face or body, and may not realize they are doing

miscommunication Failure to communicate information clearly or correctly

monotone A way of talking without lowering or raising the sound of your voice

nonverbal communication Using your body to send messages without speaking

oral communication Sharing ideas, information, and feelings through spoken words; also called verbal communication

patents Gets exclusive rights from a government to make, use, and sell an invention for a set period of time

reflecting statement A statement that repeats a speaker's thoughts and feelings in your own words, and helps you understand their message

social media Websites and applications that allow people to create profiles and join online communities so they can connect with others and share information

verbal communication Sharing ideas, information, and feelings through spoken words; also called oral communication

visual communication Using pictures, signs, and other visual aids to share ideas and information

written communication Sharing ideas, information, and feelings in writing

LEARNING MORE

Books

Beyond Texting: The Fine Art of Face-to-Face Communication for Teenagers by Debra Fine. Canon Publishers, 2014.

Communication Then and Now by Bobbie Kalman. Crabtree Publishing Company, 2014.

Social Media: Like It or Leave It by Rebecca Rowell. Compass Point Books, 2015.

Writing Letters (Write Right!) by Benjamin Proudfit. Gareth Stevens Publishing, 2014.

You Wouldn't Want to Live Without Cell Phones! by Jim Pipe. Scholastic, 2014.

Websites

Cyberbullying
www.stopbullying.gov
Visit this website to learn about cyberbullying and how to prevent and report it.

#InstaFame: Positive Social Media
www.hashtaginstafame.com/positive-use-of-social-media/
This website shows students how they can put a positive spin on social media use.

Khan Academy
www.khanacademy.org
Watch this site's YouTube videos to learn about communication and countless other subjects.

Pew Research Center
www.pewinternet.org
This informative site provides statistics and highlights trends in communication and other fields.

Skype in the Classroom
https://education.microsoft.com/skypeintheclassroom
Use this website at school with your teachers and classmates to play Mystery Skype, talk with guest speakers, and take virtual field trips.

Ted Ed: How Miscommunication Happens
http://ed.ted.com/lessons/how-to-avoid-miscommunication-katherine-hampsten
This video lesson teaches how miscommunication happens—and how to avoid it.

INDEX

About the Author

Robin Johnson has been communicating since she was born. She graduated from Queen's University with a degree in English and Film Studies, and she has now written more than 60 nonfiction books for children. When she's not communicating at work, Robin spends her free time sweet talking her husband and two sons, and sharing her bright ideas with anyone who will listen.